Wedding Memories

Illustrated by Leesa Whitten

Text and Illustrations copyright © 1990
by Beverly Clark
ISBN 0-934081-05-0

Published in 1990 by
Wilshire Publications, Carpinteria

Printed in Hong Kong

Distributed by:

Beverly Clark Collection
Wilshire Publications
1120 Mark Avenue
Carpinteria, CA 93013

Publishers Group West
4065 Hollis, Emeryville, CA 94608

Wedding Memories

By

Beverly Clark

Illustrated by Leesa Whitten

Wilshire Publications, Publisher, Carpinteria

A wedding begins
a whole new world,
as two hearts pledge one love
and two lives join
in one dream for the future.

K. Rutz

The Marriage

The Marriage of

_____

and

_____

Who Were United in Marriage

on _____

at _____

The Bride

My maiden name _____

I was born on _____

My birthplace _____

Photo

The Groom

His full name _____

He was born on _____

His birthplace _____

Photo

_____
mother's father

born on _____

at _____

_____
mother's mother

born on _____

at _____

_____
father's father

born on _____

at _____

_____
father's mother

born on _____

at _____

_____
his father

born on _____

at _____

_____
his mother

born on _____

at _____

_____
Groom

Family Tree

_____
mother's father
born on _____
at _____

_____
father's father
born on _____
at _____

_____
mother's mother
born on _____
at _____

_____
father's mother
born on _____
at _____

_____
my father
born on _____
at _____

_____
my mother
born on _____
at _____

_____
Bride

Our Family

My mother's heritage is _____

_____

_____

My father's heritage is _____

_____

_____

My parents first met at _____

_____ on _____

Their first date _____

_____

They were married on _____

     at _____

     in _____

She was _____ years old and he was _____

_____

Their first home was _____

_____

History

His mother's heritage is _____

_____

_____

His father's heritage is _____

_____

_____

His parents first met at _____

_____ on _____

Their first date _____

_____

They were married on _____

at _____

in _____

She was _____ years old and he was _____

_____

Their first home was _____

_____

We First Met

*She is beautiful and therefore
to be wooed,
She is a woman, and therefore
to be won.*

William Shakespeare

We first met on _____ at _____

_____

We were introduced by _____

_____

I was wearing _____

_____

He was wearing _____

_____

My first impression of him _____

_____

_____

_____

His first impression of me _____

_____

Our First Date

*Who ever loved that
loved not at first sight?*

Christopher Marlowe

Our first date was on _____

_____

_____

He took me to _____

_____

_____

Reflections of our first date _____

_____

_____

_____

_____

_____

_____

_____

Our Love Grew

Love looks not with the eyes,
but with the mind,
And therefore is winged Cupid
painted blind.

William Shakespeare

Our first kiss _____

_____

_____

My feelings for him grew because _____

_____

_____

The most romantic evening we spent was _____

_____

_____

_____

_____

The things we enjoy doing together _____

_____

_____

_____

_____

_____

Places we've been together _____

_____

_____

_____

_____

_____

I knew he was the one for me when _____

_____

_____

_____

_____

I will never forget _____

_____

_____

_____

_____

_____

The Proposal

Come live with me and be my love
And we will all the pleasures prove.

Christopher Marlowe

He proposed to me on _____

at _____

while we were _____

_____

The words he said _____

_____

_____

_____

I replied _____

_____

_____

_____

He gave me _____

_____ to commemorate our engagement.

We first told _____

_____

_____

Memories of the proposal _____

_____

_____

_____

_____

_____

We announced our engagement by _____

_____

_____

_____

_____

Our Engagement

I have nothing to share with you
but my life.
Peter McWilliams

Our engagement was celebrated by a _____

_____ on _____

at _____

and was attended by _____

_____

_____

Other celebrations given in our honor _____

_____

_____

_____

Engagement gifts we received _____

_____

_____

_____

_____

Engagement Announcement

Our Wedding Plans

We selected the date of _____

    to be married at _____

_____

_____

We were married by _____

    who is _____

_____

My maid or matron of honor was _____

_____

who I have known for _____ years _____

_____

My bridesmaids were _____

_____

_____

_____

_____

My fiancé's best man was _____

_____

who he has known for _____ years _____

His groomsmen were _____

_____

_____

_____

_____

Other members of the bridal party were _____

_____

_____

The reception was a _____

held at _____

_____

The reception colors were _____

_____

My floral arrangements were _____

_____ by _____

Music was played by _____

_____

Our photographer was _____

_____

My Bridal Shower

A shower was given for me by _____

on _____

at _____

The shower theme was _____

_____

guests who attended	gifts	thank you

My Bridal Shower

A shower was given for me by _____

on _____

at _____

The shower theme was _____

_____

guests who attended   gifts   thank you

_____   _____   _____

_____   _____   _____

_____   _____   _____

_____   _____   _____

_____   _____   _____

_____   _____   _____

_____   _____   _____

_____   _____   _____

_____   _____   _____

_____   _____   _____

_____   _____   _____

_____   _____   _____

_____   _____   _____

_____   _____   _____

_____   _____   _____

_____   _____   _____

Celebrations

The event _____

Hosted by _____

Date _____

Time _____

Place _____

Guests who attended _____

_____

_____

_____

_____

_____

_____

_____

_____

_____

Memorable moments _____

_____

_____

Celebrations

The event _____

Hosted by _____

Date _____

Time _____

Place _____

Guests who attended _____

_____

_____

_____

_____

_____

_____

_____

_____

_____

Memorable moments _____

_____

_____

_____

My Bridesmaids' Luncheon

Date _____

Time _____

Place _____

Guests who attended _____

_____

_____

_____

_____

_____

_____

_____

_____

_____

_____

Gifts to the bridesmaids were _____

_____

_____

_____

_____

The Bachelor Party

Was given by _____

Date _____

Time _____

Place _____

Guests who attended _____

_____

_____

_____

_____

_____

_____

_____

_____

_____

_____

_____

_____

Gifts to the groom's attendants were _____

_____

_____

_____

The Rehearsal

The rehearsal was held at _____

on _____ at _____ o'clock.

_____

_____

The rehearsal dinner was given by _____

_____

and held at _____

_____

The menu included _____

_____

_____

_____

Speeches and toasts were given by _____

_____

_____

_____

_____

Rehearsal Dinner Guests

_____

_____

_____

_____

_____

_____

_____

_____

_____

_____

_____

_____

_____

_____

_____

Wedding

My bridal gown was _____

_____

_____

_____

Purchased or made by _____

_____

My headpiece was _____

_____

I carried _____

_____

My something old was _____

_____

My something new was _____

_____

My something borrowed was _____

_____

My something blue was _____

_____

Attire

My husband wore _____

_____

with a boutonniere of _____

_____

My bridal attendants wore _____

_____

and they carried _____

_____

The grooms attendants wore _____

_____

with boutonnieres of _____

_____

My flowergirl wore _____

_____

she carried _____

_____

My ringbearer wore _____

_____

On Our Wedding Day

On our wedding day _____

_____

The weather was _____

_____

_____

The President was _____

_____

_____

The headlines were _____

_____

_____

The latest fad was _____

_____

_____

The most popular movie was _____

_____

_____

Our favorite song was _____

_____

_____

My thoughts and feelings were _____

_____

_____

_____

_____

_____

_____

_____

_____

Our Ceremony

I was escorted down the aisle by _____

_____

_____

The music we walked down the aisle to was _____

_____

_____

The ceremony was officiated by _____

_____

_____

Special readings or poems from the ceremony were _____

_____

_____

_____

_____

The vows we exchanged were _____

_____

_____

_____

_____

_____

_____

The most sentimental moment was _____

_____

_____

_____

Unexpected moments that made the ceremony memorable, were

_____

_____

_____

_____

_____

As husband and wife the song we walked out to was _____

_____

_____

_____

_____

Bride's Family

_____   _____
Bride's mother   Bride's father

To Our Daughter _____

_____

_____

_____

_____

_____   _____
Mother's mother   Father's mother

_____   _____
Mother's father   Father's father

Bride's Attendants

_____   _____

_____   _____

_____   _____

_____   _____

_____   _____

Groom's Family

_____ _____
Groom's mother   Groom's father

To Our Son _____

_____

_____

_____

_____

_____ _____
Mother's mother   Father's mother

_____ _____
Mother's father   Father's father

Groom's Attendants

_____ _____

_____ _____

_____ _____

_____ _____

Guests

Names   Thoughts

_____   _____

_____   _____

_____   _____

_____   _____

_____   _____

_____   _____

_____   _____

_____   _____

_____   _____

_____   _____

_____   _____

_____   _____

_____   _____

_____   _____

_____   _____

_____   _____

_____   _____

_____   _____

_____   _____

Guests

Names   Thoughts

_____   _____

_____   _____

_____   _____

_____   _____

_____   _____

_____   _____

_____   _____

_____   _____

_____   _____

_____   _____

_____   _____

_____   _____

_____   _____

_____   _____

_____   _____

_____   _____

_____   _____

_____   _____

Guests

Names

Thoughts

Guests

Names   Thoughts

_____   _____

_____   _____

_____   _____

_____   _____

_____   _____

_____   _____

_____   _____

_____   _____

_____   _____

_____   _____

_____   _____

_____   _____

_____   _____

_____   _____

_____   _____

_____   _____

_____   _____

Guests

Names *Thoughts*

_____ _____

_____ _____

_____ _____

_____ _____

_____ _____

_____ _____

_____ _____

_____ _____

_____ _____

_____ _____

_____ _____

_____ _____

_____ _____

_____ _____

_____ _____

_____ _____

_____ _____

Guests

Names   Thoughts

_____   _____

_____   _____

_____   _____

_____   _____

_____   _____

_____   _____

_____   _____

_____   _____

_____   _____

_____   _____

_____   _____

_____   _____

_____   _____

_____   _____

_____   _____

_____   _____

_____   _____

Guests

Names

Thoughts

Guests

Names   Thoughts

_____ _____
_____ _____
_____ _____
_____ _____
_____ _____
_____ _____
_____ _____
_____ _____
_____ _____
_____ _____
_____ _____
_____ _____
_____ _____
_____ _____
_____ _____
_____ _____
_____ _____

Guests

Names

Thoughts

_____   _____

_____   _____

_____   _____

_____   _____

_____   _____

_____   _____

_____   _____

_____   _____

_____   _____

_____   _____

_____   _____

_____   _____

_____   _____

_____   _____

_____   _____

_____   _____

_____   _____

_____   _____

_____   _____

Guests

Names   Thoughts

_____   _____
_____   _____
_____   _____
_____   _____
_____   _____
_____   _____
_____   _____
_____   _____
_____   _____
_____   _____
_____   _____
_____   _____
_____   _____
_____   _____
_____   _____
_____   _____
_____   _____
_____   _____
_____   _____
_____   _____

Guests

Names

Thoughts

The Reception

Appetizers

_____

First Course

_____

_____

Main Course

_____

_____

_____

Wines

_____

Dessert

_____

Wedding Cake

_____

The Reception

Our first dance was to _____

_____

_____

The first toast was given by _____

_____

who said _____

_____

_____

_____

The funniest toast was given by _____

_____

who said _____

_____

_____

_____

Other traditional wedding rituals we did _____

_____

_____

_____

_____

The Reception

Special moments worth remembering _____

_____

_____

_____

_____

After we cut the cake _____

_____

_____

My bouquet was caught by _____

_____

her reaction _____

_____

My garter was caught by _____

_____

his reaction _____

_____

We left the reception at _____

I was wearing _____

_____

we left in _____

_____

Our Wedding

Invitation

Wedding

Photographs

Wedding
Mementos

Wedding Mementos

Wedding Gifts

My gift to my husband was _____

_____

His gift to me was _____

_____

gifts	*Given by*	*acknowledged*
_____	_____	_____
_____	_____	_____
_____	_____	_____
_____	_____	_____
_____	_____	_____
_____	_____	_____
_____	_____	_____
_____	_____	_____
_____	_____	_____
_____	_____	_____
_____	_____	_____
_____	_____	_____
_____	_____	_____
_____	_____	_____
_____	_____	_____

Wedding Gifts

gifts	Given by	acknowledged

Wedding Gifts

gifts   Given by   acknowledged

Wedding Gifts

gifts   Given by   acknowledged

Wedding Gifts

gifts   Given by   acknowledged

_____   _____   _____

_____   _____   _____

_____   _____   _____

_____   _____   _____

_____   _____   _____

_____   _____   _____

_____   _____   _____

_____   _____   _____

_____   _____   _____

_____   _____   _____

_____   _____   _____

_____   _____   _____

_____   _____   _____

_____   _____   _____

_____   _____   _____

_____   _____   _____

_____   _____   _____

_____   _____   _____

_____   _____   _____

_____   _____   _____

Wedding Gifts

gifts   Given by   acknowledged

_____

_____

_____

_____

_____

_____

_____

_____

_____

_____

_____

_____

_____

_____

_____

_____

_____

_____

_____

_____

Wedding Gifts

gifts   Given by   acknowledged

_____ _____ _____

_____ _____ _____

_____ _____ _____

_____ _____ _____

_____ _____ _____

_____ _____ _____

_____ _____ _____

_____ _____ _____

_____ _____ _____

_____ _____ _____

_____ _____ _____

_____ _____ _____

_____ _____ _____

_____ _____ _____

_____ _____ _____

_____ _____ _____

_____ _____ _____

_____ _____ _____

_____ _____ _____

Wedding Gifts

gifts	Given by	acknowledged

Wedding Gifts

gifts	Given by	acknowledged

Wedding Gifts

gifts	Given by	acknowledged
_____	_____	_____
_____	_____	_____
_____	_____	_____
_____	_____	_____
_____	_____	_____
_____	_____	_____
_____	_____	_____
_____	_____	_____
_____	_____	_____
_____	_____	_____
_____	_____	_____
_____	_____	_____
_____	_____	_____
_____	_____	_____
_____	_____	_____
_____	_____	_____
_____	_____	_____
_____	_____	_____
_____	_____	_____
_____	_____	_____
_____	_____	_____

Our Honeymoon

Our wedding night was spent at _____

_____

_____

We honeymooned from _____

to _____

_____

We went to _____

_____

_____

We arrived by _____

_____

_____

Our most romantic moment _____

_____

_____

Our funniest experience _____

_____

_____

_____

Our most romantic dinner was _____

_____

_____

Our fondest memories are _____

_____

_____

_____

_____

_____

_____

Our First Home

And I will make thee beds of roses
And a thousand fragrant posies.

Christopher Marlowe

Our first home was _____

_____

the address was _____

_____

we moved in on _____

_____

We decorated it _____

_____

_____

Our first household purchase together was _____

_____

The first piece of furniture we bought was _____

_____

_____

We were given _____

Our First Year

*Each day can bring you lovely times
with happy things to do,
times to dream and time to try
to make those dreams come true...*

Rachel Davis

Our first holiday together was _____

_____

    it was spent by _____

Our first dinner party was _____

_____

_____

Our fondest memory was _____

_____

_____

Our future dreams include _____

_____

_____

_____

Our First Anniversary

Our first anniversary was celebrated by _____

_____

_____

My gift to him was _____

_____

His gift to me was _____

_____

The fondest memory of our first year _____

_____

_____

_____

_____

_____